YOU ARE
P L A I N
as
DIRT

What Type of Soil Is Your Heart?

Andrew Wommack

Published in partnership between Andrew Wommack Ministries and Harrison House Publishers.
Woodland Park, CO 80863 – Shippensburg, PA 17257

ISBN 13 TP: 978-1-59548-592-2

For Worldwide Distribution, Printed in the USA

1 2 3 4 5 6 / 26 25 24 23

Contents

Introduction 1

Reading the Bible 3

Bible Study Methods 6

The Foundation of the Word 9

The Word Is Seed 12

The Earth Brings Forth 15

Parable of the Sower 18

Sowing by the Wayside 21

Sowing on Stony Ground 24

Sowing Among Thorns 27

Sowing into Good Soil 30

Seed, Time, and Harvest 33

Putting Down Roots 37

Sustaining Spiritual Growth 40

Reaping a Harvest 43

Conclusion 47

Receive Jesus as Your Savior 51

Receive the Holy Spirit 53

Call for Prayer 55

About the Author 57

Introduction

Jesus often used parables to communicate spiritual truths in a way that could be commonly understood. In the parable of the sower (Mark 4:1–20), Jesus taught that the Word of God is like a seed, and our heart is like soil. Jesus told His disciples that if they couldn't understand that one parable, they wouldn't be able to understand any other parables. There's something in that single parable that shows us how valuable and powerful the Word of God really is when it is sown into our hearts. Yet, sad to say, many Christians just don't make time to study the Bible.

Are you unable to commit yourself to reading the Bible on a regular basis? Do you find there are so many other things that seem to get in the way of studying God's Word? At the same time, do you also struggle in the areas of health, finances, and relationships?

What if I told you that everything you needed to be successful—to be whole physically, financially, and in every other area of your life—is already deposited in your born-again spirit? And what if I told you the only thing you needed to activate it was to sow the seed of God's Word? Now, how do you think your life would change if you committed yourself to studying the Bible on a regular basis? I'll tell you, the Word of God is the most essential thing you need in your life, both spiritually and physically. It has the power to transform the world!

You may already be familiar with my teaching *Effortless Change*, which is one of the most important things I've ever taught. It has become a foundational truth for many people and covers many of the topics I discuss in this booklet.

But even though I've already taught many of these things, the Lord recently gave me some new revelation I'm calling *Plain as Dirt*. It's essentially the same truth, but just presented in a different way. And it is powerful!

In this booklet, I'll be sharing valuable insights into how to study the Bible and the difference it makes in your life when you do. The Word of God is an incorruptible seed that brings forth fruit when planted in your heart. Learn how to let God's Word change your life for the better and let it activate what you already have in your born-again spirit!

Reading the Bible

All scripture is *given by inspiration of God, and is profitable for doctrine, for reproof, for correction, for instruction in righteousness: that the man of God may be perfect, throughly furnished unto all good works.*

2 Timothy 3:16–17

I know there are many of you reading this who love God but may have never read through the whole Bible.

First-year students in my class at Charis Bible College are required to read through the Bible during the school year. In fact, it is 20 percent of their course grade. I think people who come to Bible college should actually read the Bible, amen!

For whatever reason, the church has been making converts but not disciples. By Jesus' own definition, a disciple is a person who continues *in His Word* until they are free (John 8:31–32). The church has not emphasized God's Word nearly enough, and it's caused millions of people who claim to be Christians to just not let the Bible get in the way of what they believe.

Several years ago, I had a student at Charis Bible College tell me that the school had radically changed her life. She said she was an extreme liberal on social issues when she first came, but by graduation, she had become so conservative that many in her own family had nearly disowned her because of her beliefs.

I asked this woman to explain how she had been able to say she loved the Lord, and yet also had been for abortion, homosexuality, transgenderism, and all sorts of other ungodly things. She said, "I loved God, but I didn't love the Bible. When I came to Charis, I learned to love the Word of God, and that changed everything. You can't love God's Word and be a liberal."

My friend David Barton of WallBuilders said there has been a dramatic decline in the number of people who are regular readers of the Bible.[1] The youth of this nation used to learn God's Word in our schools. The *New England Primer*, which was used for over a century, was full of God's Word. Even those who didn't embrace all the truths presented were aware of what God's Word said, and it had a restraining influence.

But because many people have forsaken the biblical standard of truth, people today can't even figure out which bathroom to use. I once heard that over 90 percent of pastors believed they were in a position of influence to provide their church with instructions on every issue facing us today. But less than 10 percent of those same pastors believed their people were well-equipped to speak on those same issues.[2] This is part of the reason I require every Charis student to read through the Bible in one year.

As Christians, it's important for us to sow the seed of God's Word into our hearts so we can bear fruit (Gal. 5:22–23) and be ready to give an answer to every man that asks about the hope that is in us (1 Pet. 3:15). There is a world dying for lack of answers to the issues they face, and I believe the Word of God has them.

Bible Study Methods

I teach on four different methods of Bible study: systematic, topical, meditation, and word study.

The simplest and most foundational of the four is **systematic Bible study**, where you just read through Scripture. Because all Scripture is given by inspiration of God, there is no way you can receive any benefit if you haven't even read it. So, you've got to just systematically read through the Scripture beginning at Genesis and go all the way to Revelation.

But the Bible is a big book, and it takes a long time to read it all the way through. If all you did was just systematically study, by the time you get to the end, you would need to go back and start over to refresh yourself. It could also take you twenty or thirty years to get all that information and connect the dots.

Another method is **topical study**. This is where you study on topics like healing, prosperity, deliverance, or relationships. If you take the scriptures that deal with those things, pull them all together, and meditate on them, you can get your faith built up quickly. But there's also a danger to that. If you only study the topics that you're interested in, you could get really strong in one area and yet be deficient in another because it's not what you are studying. That's what happened to me!

> Because all Scripture is given by inspiration of God, there is no way you can receive any benefit if you haven't even read it.

When I got turned on to the Lord and just began immersing myself in God's Word, I focused on healing. I got really strong in that area, and we saw some miraculous things, but our ministry was nearly destroyed because I didn't have a revelation on prosperity. So, I took the Word of God, and for two years, I focused on some things until prosperity changed our ministry. (I'll go into more detail on that later.) Now we're on television all around the world, and we are adding to our Charis Bible College campus in Woodland Park, Colorado. Those things probably would not have happened if I just stayed focused on healing.

Meditation is another way of studying the Word. This is one of the most important forms of Bible study there is. Psalm 1:2 says, a man's *"delight* is *in the law of the* Lord; *and in his law doth he meditate day and night."* Now look at Psalm 2:1. It says, *"Why do the heathen rage, and the people imagine a vain thing?"* Did you know the word *meditate* in Psalm 1:2 and the word *imagine* in Psalm 2:1 are translated from the exact same Hebrew word?[3]

The same part of you that meditates is the same part of you that worries (imagines negative things). I bet every person reading this booklet has had something happen, financially, physically, or in a relationship, and let their imagination run wild about it. That's worrying! And yet, you're able to go to work and still do a good job, but your mind is never off of that problem that you're dealing with. Worry is just meditation in a negative way.

In the same way, you can meditate on the Word of God. You can study the Bible, close it, and then meditate the rest of the day on what you read. Let the Word paint a positive picture on the inside of you instead of worrying about what your doctor or banker said to you.

That brings us to the study of individual words, like what I just did in Psalm 1:2 and Psalm 2:1, with the words *meditate and imagine*. A **word study** will show they are taken from the same word in the Hebrew language. That will help you understand what meditation is because you will see that it involves your imagination.

The Foundation of the Word

You may have heard me tell the story of how I really got turned on to the Lord, March 23, 1968. That

Saturday night, in a pastor's study in Arlington, Texas, I had a supernatural experience that changed my life.

For four and a half months, I was caught up in the supernatural love of God. It was powerful and things have never been the same since. But after a time, the emotional feeling that accompanied my experience wore off. My circumstances were about to change dramatically, and I had to turn to something more than a feeling to sustain me.

Thankfully, I was raised in a church that taught the importance of learning the Word of God, so I had been studying my Bible on a regular basis. But now I needed the foundation of God's Word more than ever. Not long after my supernatural experience with God, I left college, was drafted into the army, and deployed to Vietnam. When we received our orders to ship out, a chaplain ministered to a group of us and said, "The military is like a fire, and it will melt you, but you get to choose what mold you're poured into." What he said really blessed me in that moment, so I decided to make it a positive experience.

But not everything that happened to me was enjoyable! When I was in basic training, I nearly died from being exposed to CS gas (also known as tear gas). I'll spare you the details of what happened; but, I'll tell you, it was bad!

During my first week after we arrived in Vietnam, we spent a couple of days getting checked in and going through additional training. They announced that we were going to go through a gas chamber, and it would be filled with CS gas so we could practice putting on our masks and preparing ourselves in case we were attacked. I remember telling the Lord that I just couldn't go through CS gas training again and that I'd do anything to avoid it.

At breakfast the next day, they asked for a volunteer. Now, one of the things I learned early on in the army is not to volunteer for anything. That's just not a smart thing to do! But I figured that even if they used me for target practice, it would be better than going through a gas chamber. So, I volunteered!

As it turned out, what they did was make me bunker guard. That meant while everybody else was going through the gas chamber and getting exposed to CS gas, I was just making sure that nobody came in and stole anybody else's belongings.

So, I just lay on my bunk and studied the Bible. It was awesome! Not only did I not get gassed, I got into the Word of God. And on that day, I read a passage of scripture from the Gospel of Mark that just made a huge impact on me.

The Word Is Seed

Before I share with you what the Lord revealed to me on that day in Vietnam, I want us to take a closer look at what Jesus had to say about seed and soil—the Word and your heart.

If you study all four of the Gospels—Matthew, Mark, Luke, and John—you will see that Jesus taught thirteen parables in one day. The Lord taught three parables in the fourth chapter of Mark, which illustrate the Word is to the kingdom of God what a natural seed is to a harvest.

First Peter 1:23 says,

Being born again, not of corruptible seed, but of incorruptible, by the word of God, which liveth and abideth for ever.

According to this verse, the Word of God is a seed, an incorruptible seed. That word *seed* is translated from the Greek word *spora*.[4] It is related to the word *sperma*,[5] which is where we get our word *sperm*, referring to the seed a man sows into a woman to conceive a child.

Conception cannot take place without first planting the seed. Now, I'm not going to explain how all that works, but it's safe to say there has only been one virgin birth, and you aren't going to be the second! I talk to people all the time who pray and believe for God to do something in their lives but remain frustrated with the results. It's because they are missing the seeds of conception; they just don't know God's Word. To conceive and give birth from your spirit, you must first plant God's Word like a seed in your heart.

God's kingdom operates on laws, like the laws that govern the fruit-bearing process of a seed. And this is precisely the reason most people don't see God's best come to pass in their lives. They think that since God loves them, He will just grant their request regardless of whether they put the seed of God's Word to work or not. But God has *already* done His part. He has given us the Word! For example, the Lord doesn't give us money directly. Deuteronomy 8:18 says that the Lord gives us power to get wealth. The power is in His promises—His Word. As we plant those promises in our hearts, the truth of His Word germinates, and prosperity comes.

> To conceive and give birth from your spirit, you must first plant God's Word like a seed in your heart.

Likewise, the proper way to get healed is to take God's promises of healing and plant them in our hearts until they release their life-giving power into our physical bodies.

I just can't tell you how important it is that you know God's Word and that you plant that seed in your heart. It could mean the difference between prosperity and poverty, or even life and death. But the seed can do nothing without soil. Scientists have actually taken seeds found at ancient historical sites and planted them. Once those seeds that laid dormant for thousands of years were put in soil, all of a sudden, they sprang up and produced.[6] That's powerful!

The Earth Brings Forth

And God said, Let the earth bring forth grass, the herb yielding seed, and *the fruit tree yielding fruit after his kind, whose seed* is *in itself, upon the earth: and it was so.*

Genesis 1:11

Notice it says that the earth brought forth plants and trees. They were already in the earth, and God brought all of these things—everything that we see—out of the ground with His Word.

One time at a meeting in Kansas City, a man came up and told me I was "plain as dirt." Now, I don't think he meant that as a compliment, but dirt is miraculous. What is in the ground—plain old dirt—has the potential to produce everything around us. Did you know everything you see above ground was at one time in the ground? There are things all around us made of wood, plastic, glass, and metal that were once in the ground.

In Genesis 1:24,

God said, Let the earth bring forth the living creature after his kind, cattle, and creeping thing, and beast of the earth after his kind: and it was so.

God brought all of the animals out of the ground. Did you know that animals as different as elephants, dogs, and giraffes were all once in the dirt?

Even mankind was made out of the ground. Genesis 2:7 says,

And the Lord God formed man of the dust of the ground, and breathed into his nostrils the breath of life; and man became a living soul.

Our original father came out of the ground, and so did all the animals. Giraffes, elephants, dogs, and all animals were already in the ground. They just needed the seed of God's Word to make them come alive (Gen. 1:24–25).

In Mark 4:26–28, Jesus said,

So is the kingdom of God, as if a man should cast seed into the ground; and should sleep, and rise night and day, and the seed should spring and grow up, he knoweth not how. For the earth bringeth forth fruit of herself; first the blade, then the ear, after that the full corn in the ear.

Notice He said, *"the earth brings forth fruit of herself."* That is really significant.

I've seen people hold up an apple seed, and say, "Anybody can count the number of seeds in an apple, but nobody can count the number of apples in a seed."

They're saying if you plant a seed, it will produce a tree that will produce hundreds of apples; and in each apple, there are many seeds, and so on. I understand the point that's being made, but according to Genesis 1:11–12 and Mark 4:28, seeds don't produce apples. The earth produces. The seed activates what is already in the soil. This is a different concept that I want you to consider. And if you could understand and apply it to your personal life, I believe it would just change everything!

Parable of the Sower

The first parable Jesus taught in the fourth chapter of Mark, the parable of the sower (vv. 1–20,), is the key to unlocking all the Word of God. If we don't understand these truths, Jesus said we won't understand any of His other parables (Mark 4:13). That is really significant because He's saying that if you don't understand this teaching, then you won't be able to understand any of His teachings. So, this is like a key that unlocks everything else.

In this parable, Jesus described four types of soil into which seed could be sown, but He really wasn't teaching about agriculture. When Jesus later explained the parable to His disciples, He revealed that the seed was the Word of God and that the soil was people's hearts.

The Word of God contains total power (Ps. 138:2 and Heb. 1:3), but it has to be planted in our hearts and allowed to germinate before it releases that power. The Word was the same in each situation. It was good seed—incorruptible seed (1 Pet. 1:23)—but there were different results in each case because of the condition of people's hearts.

The Word doesn't work for everyone because not everyone will allow the Word to work. What would happen if you planted a seed in your garden and then dug it up each morning to see if anything was happening? It would die and never produce fruit. You have to have faith that the seed is doing what God created it to do.

Some people put God's Word in their hearts for a day or two, but if they don't see fruit almost immediately, they dig up the seed through their words and actions and wonder why it didn't work. You have to leave it in the ground. I believe we can take the supernatural words of God—the seed of miracles we need—and meditate on them until we can see the result in our hearts. Those who will place His words in their hearts and allow those seeds to take root and sprout will in time see the manifestation of what they believe and speak.

> **The Word doesn't work for everyone because not everyone will allow the Word to work.**

The variable in this parable is the condition of these hearts. God's Word is always the same. It has the same potential in every heart. In Jesus' time, seeds weren't planted in neat rows by machinery like they are today. Seed was sown by hand and thrown across the ground by a sower. Even though the soil in a field was prepared for planting, the nature of sowing by hand was such that some seed would fall on ground that just wasn't conducive to good growth.

As Jesus gave the parable, He described each kind of soil as it related to people's hearts. First, there was the ground by the wayside (Mark 4:4), then the stony ground (Mark 4:5–6), the seeds sown among thorns (Mark 4:7), and the good soil that yielded thirty-, sixty-, or a hundredfold (Mark 4:8).

Sowing by the Wayside

And it came to pass, as he sowed, some fell by the way side, and the fowls of the air came and devoured it up.

Mark 4:4

The first type of soil described by Jesus is that found along the wayside. In Jesus' time, this wayside ground was where people or animals walked, so it was hard and packed down. In the same way today, a road that goes past a field may be paved with dirt, but wheels from cars and trucks pack down the ground so that nothing will grow in it. If seeds fall on that soil, they can be snatched up by birds because they are just lying on the surface and not putting down roots.

A heart represented by the wayside ground is one that has no understanding of God's Word (Matt. 13:19). The Word never gets inside of the heart but lays on the surface where it's easily stolen away by the devil (v. 15). Jesus said that Satan has the ability to steal this Word from those who understand it not. Therefore, understanding is the first step in getting God's Word down on the inside of us.

Ephesians 4:17b–18 says,

Walk not as other Gentiles walk, in the vanity of their mind, having the understanding darkened, being alienated from the life of God through the ignorance that is in them, because of the blindness of their heart.

That's referring to a person who doesn't have a covenant with God, who can't perceive or understand, and is far from Him due to their ignorance and spiritual blindness. If you cannot understand, then the seed of God's Word cannot be released in your life. Like hard, packed-down ground, you may have a hardened heart.

A hard heart is characterized by an inability to perceive spiritually. And when spiritual things are perceived, a hard heart will keep a person from understanding the few things they can perceive. They might see what the Lord is trying to show them, but they can't get a hold of it in a way that they can apply it to their life.

When people are hardhearted toward God, it's like they are spiritually blind and deaf. They just can't see spiritual truth or hear the Lord speak to them. And they can't remember. Not remembering is a major indication of the condition of their hearts. God made us so that we can protect our hearts by shutting out unwanted influences. It was meant to be a positive thing, but because we haven't understood this, what God meant for good has actually worked against us. People are shutting out the Word of God; and through lack of understanding, they can't receive that seed.

The only one of these four types of ground, or hearts, where Satan has free access to steal away the Word is this first one—where there is no understanding.

Therefore, understanding is the first step in getting the Word of God to germinate in us.

Sowing on Stony Ground

And some fell on stony ground, where it had not much earth; and immediately it sprang up, because it had no depth of earth: but when the sun was up, it was scorched; and because it had no root, it withered away.

Mark 4:5–6

The second type of soil was stony and shallow, meaning roots wouldn't be able to go deep enough to sustain a plant.

This stony ground represents a person who understands God's Word and is excited about it but doesn't take the time to get it rooted inside (vv. 16–17). In that case, the Word does germinate, but it doesn't produce fruit because it won't have a good root system. Roots develop underground, out of sight. Most people want the visible results of fruit, but they don't want to develop the root system necessary to produce and sustain the fruit.

A seed that germinates in shallow earth will put all its energies into growth above ground because there is nowhere else for its growth to go. So, at first, it looks better than the seed that is putting its effort into building a good root system. But when the sun starts drying out the plant, the root system isn't there to sustain it; and it will wither and die.

> Most people want the visible results of fruit, but they don't want to develop the root system necessary to produce and sustain the fruit.

In a similar way, someone who isn't rooted in the Word of God will wither and fall away when persecution or criticism comes (vv. 16–17). The Lord showed me this when we were being persecuted in the Baptist church, early on in our ministry.

We would regularly attend Kenneth Copeland's meetings in Fort Worth, Texas, once a month for about eighteen months; and I'd get fired up about what I was learning about faith. So, I'd come back to my Baptist church, and I'd go to preaching these things. For the first week or two, we would see people saved, delivered, and healed. We were seeing miracles happen and it was awesome!

Then, there'd be criticism, and the pastor would call me in to say, "You aren't preaching out of the quarterly, and you aren't preaching Baptist doctrine." So, by the third or the fourth week, I'd be teaching the same things, but nothing would happen. Nobody was getting set free. People would even fall asleep when I was preaching. Then I'd go back and hear Kenneth Copeland at the next meeting, and I'd get fired up again. I'd come back to my church, and for a week or two, it would be good; and then the whole cycle repeated itself. It was so predictable that I actually got to anticipating it.

I prayed, "God, what's going on?" So, the Lord showed me that I didn't have root in myself (Mark 4:17). I was just quoting Kenneth Copeland, but the

Word was not getting into my heart as a seed and taking root. It wasn't my revelation.

Now, there can be visible results in a person's life who only listens to someone else minister the Word. But when things get tough, only the Word that has deep roots in our hearts will bear fruit. From that time on, I've never had to quote somebody else. I may hear somebody else say something good, but I meditate on the Word until that truth becomes mine. It gets rooted in me so that persecution and criticism just won't affect me.

Sowing Among Thorns

And some fell among thorns, and the thorns grew up, and choked it, and it yielded no fruit.

Mark 4:7

The third kind of soil mentioned in this parable concerns thorns choking out or restricting the ability of other plants to grow and produce fruit.

This type of ground represents those who are distracted and deceived by worldly things (Mark 4:18–19). These are people who have received God's Word and committed themselves to it to the degree that they are able to remain faithful in persecution. However, by being preoccupied with the affairs of this life, the Word sown in their hearts is choked, and no fruit is produced. Just as weeds in a garden will steal nutrients and starve the plants, so the pleasures of this life—if allowed to dominate people's thinking—will stop the fruit that the Word would have produced.

Throughout history, the church has always grown in size and strength during persecution. This is because during persecution, we get our priorities straight. We realize our life is in Jesus (John 14:6) and not in things (Luke 12:15), and we focus all of our attention on the Lord.

However, prosperity has been far more damaging to the body of Christ for the exact reason stated here in this verse. God wants to bless His children with things (Ps. 35:27; Matt. 6:33; and 1 Tim. 6:17), but a preoccupation with these things will choke God's Word and make it unfruitful. If we would follow God's formula for prosperity found in Matthew 6:19–34, we could have the Word bring forth fruit and enjoy the physical blessings of this life too.

The point being made is that we only have so much attention to give. If we want fruitfulness, we need to focus on the Word and not other things that can pre-occupy us. Just as the earth only has so many nutrients and weeds take away nourishment that could be going to the desired plant, so all the things of this world will steal energy from us that could be going into the Word of God.

Notice that these aren't necessarily bad things. We have to attend to the affairs of this life to a degree. But there has to be a proper balance between job, family, leisure, and the Word. We don't strike this balance once and are through with it. This is something that constantly varies based on our seasons of life. The only way to maintain the proper balance is to maintain a deep and meaningful relationship with the Lord. He will reveal to us any time we begin to be too focused on something other than Him (Phil. 3:15).

The strength of a laser lies in its focus. If the focus is diffused, the laser ceases to be powerful. Likewise, the power of the Christian is amplified by a single focus (Phil. 3:13). The way to destroy a man's vision is to give him two, which is really the meaning of the word "division."

Sowing into Good Soil

And other fell on good ground, and did yield fruit that sprang up and increased; and brought forth, some thirty, and some sixty, and some an hundred.

Mark 4:8

The thing that made this ground good, in contrast with the three other types of ground, is not that it had more rocks, thorns, or other things, but rather that it had less. It had less weeds and fewer rocks to drain the nutrients.

Many times, we feel that we just don't have what it takes to become fruitful, but the truth is that any of us can see God's Word produce in our lives if we root out all the contrary things. Good ground doesn't just happen. It has to be cultivated. This is the reason only one out of four kinds of soil in Jesus' parable brought forth fruit.

It takes a lot of effort and diligence to be a fruitful Christian. It also takes a lot of patience. The Christian life is not like a 100-yard dash but rather a twenty-six-mile marathon. It takes time to become a fruitful Christian. It's quicker and easier to raise weeds than it is to raise tomatoes or corn. So, for your heart to be good ground, it takes eliminating preoccupation with the things of the world and placing more focus on the Lord.

In this whole parable, the Word was the catalyst that produced fruit. It was what was in the ground that allowed it to grow. If we will simply put God's Word in our hearts, protect it, and give it priority in our lives, the soil will bring forth fruit of itself.

Satan has deceived many of us into thinking that we don't have the talents or abilities to be fruitful Christians, but we are not the ones who bring forth fruit. It's God's Word planted in our hearts. When we protect the Word sown in our hearts, it will do the rest.

Good ground doesn't just happen. It has to be cultivated.

Even among those who were fruitful, there were varying degrees of fruitfulness. But this wasn't dictated by the person who sowed the Word. It's all about the condition of the soil it is sown in. God's Word has the same potential in every situation. It's not the Word that is the variable, but rather the condition of the heart that is receiving it.

Jesus compared the kingdom of God to a seed and our hearts to soil. Now, the significance of that is, if He had compared the kingdom of God to some man-made system like school, well then, it can be cheated. You can cheat on a test. People can load things in their short-term memory and pass a test, and yet never really learn the material.

You can cram for an exam, but you can't cram for a harvest. The reason Jesus used the picture of a seed to describe the kingdom of God is because it's part of how God designed things. There is seed, time, and harvest—there are steps and stages to growth.

Seed, Time, and Harvest

So is the kingdom of God, as if a man should cast seed into the ground; and should sleep, and rise night and day, and the seed should spring and grow up, he knoweth not how. For the earth bringeth forth fruit of herself; first the blade, then the ear, after that the full corn in the ear. But when the fruit is brought forth, immediately he putteth in the sickle, because the harvest is come.

Mark 4:26–29

The Greek word *automatos*, which was translated "of herself" in verse 28 is only used twice in Scripture; in this verse and Acts 12:10. It means "self-moved ('automatic'), i.e., spontaneous."[7] It's where we get our

English word *automatic.* The ground just produces fruit automatically. Likewise, our hearts are made to automatically produce whatever seed we sow in it.

And take special notice of the use of the feminine pronoun to describe our heart, or soil. Soil can't produce without seeds, but seeds can't produce without soil. Our hearts receive the seed the way a woman receives the seed of a man. Once the conception takes place, it's only a matter of time until a birth.

Just as in creation, all the animals were in the ground; but they needed the seed of God's Word to give birth to them, so everything we will ever need is already in our hearts through the new birth. We just need the incorruptible seed of God's Word to bring them to birth. Our hearts are miraculous dirt just waiting for the seed to bring out all God has put in us.

In the natural world, everything revolves around seed, time, and harvest. It's the same in the spiritual world. God's Word is the seed that, given time, produces a harvest.

But God just doesn't give you everything that you desire or need all at once. There's a growth process, and people that ignore this do it to their own detriment. It hurts you if you don't acknowledge this.

Years ago, a man who had lived his entire adult life in an assisted living facility came to Charis Bible College. His parents paid for him to be there because he wasn't mentally the way he should be.

All that time, he was fed and taken care of, never worked a job, never had a family, and never did the things adults typically do. He was in his 40s but just didn't understand the basic things of life. But he got out of there and came directly to Bible college.

I took a liking to this guy and felt like he was a diamond in the rough. So, I started teaching him from the book of Proverbs, and God started speaking to him. After a while, he got to where he was dreaming of being productive instead of just surviving and living off of other people.

Eventually this man found an abandoned hotel in Manitou Springs, Colorado, that was built in the 1800s but had burned down. It was a stone structure, but the wood was destroyed, so it was just sitting there, derelict. He found out what the building was selling for and how much it would cost to refurbish. It had more than 100 rooms in it, and he planned to rent them to Bible college students. He figured out what he could charge them, how much the payments were, and what his cash flow would be. This man had an entire prospectus made out, shared it with me, and asked, "What do you think?"

I said, "Well, it's a great plan, and you've put a lot of effort into it—I commend you for that—but I can guarantee you this is not God's will for your life." It was like I just burst his bubble! But I told him, "You're wanting to go from never having done anything to a $5 million project? It's not God."

That's when I took him to Mark 4:28 and said, "You go get a job, and you start paying your own way instead of having your parents or welfare do it; go out and do things, and then manage something. You show me some steps toward this, bring it back to me, and I'll endorse it!"

I've just learned that nobody ever goes from never having done anything to where you see this great total success. There is first a blade, then the ear, then the full corn in the ear. Things have to grow in steps and stages if you want to fulfill God's vision for your life.

A person can't just put the seed of God's Word in the ground and expect a harvest the next day. They have to give it time to sprout and grow, recognizing there are steps toward success. The first step is really to allow roots to grow to support your growth.

Putting Down Roots

When I was a kid in Arlington, Texas, our house had twenty-three pecan trees out in the yard. The pecans we didn't harvest fell to the ground and took root. My job was to pluck up seedlings before they got too big. Being a typical kid, though, I didn't want to go out there and spend my time pulling up pecan trees. I had other things to do! So, I'd ignore them.

Those pecans would get down in our grass and sprout, and I'd see them come up. But I thought, *Well, my parents can't see them*, so I let them grow. I'd wait until they got a foot tall and then my dad would drive up to the house, see them growing, and say, "You go out there and pull up those pecan trees!" By that time, those little seedlings had put down roots, and I couldn't just pull them with my hands. I had to get a shovel and dig them up.

I learned that if I waited until a pecan tree grew to be one foot tall, it already had three feet of roots below ground. There is always more root below the ground than there is growth above the ground. That's because as a plant grows, it not only needs nutrients from the ground, but it needs support so it won't fall over at the first gust of wind.

When I was in the sixth grade, I had a teacher who took two identical glass terrariums and filled one with about an inch of dirt and the other with as much as a foot of dirt. Then, he planted tomato seeds in both of them, and put those things on his desk in front of us.

They sat right next to each other. We watered those seeds exactly the same. They got the same temperature, the same sunlight, and everything was identical—except the amount of dirt in each terrarium. I sat right in the front row and looked at those things every day.

The tomato seed that was planted in the shallow earth sprung up first. It grew about an inch or two tall, but there was nothing we could see growing in the other terrarium. That thing wound up probably growing to be a foot tall before the other one even broke the ground, but it didn't have a very deep root system.

> **There is always more root below the ground than there is growth above the ground.**

Because there wasn't a depth of earth, that seed had to put all of its effort into producing something above the ground, and it couldn't sustain the growth. Eventually, it turned white and fell apart as the other one was just barely beginning to grow. But the one that had the depth of earth and put down roots grew, we wound up staking the thing. It grew to be three or four feet tall and produced tomatoes. That was quite a lesson about how a seed has to have a root to sustain its growth.

Even though it appeared big and healthy at first, there was nothing to give that first plant the stability it needed. When it had nothing to draw on, it withered and died. In the same way, I've seen ministers come on the scene, and it seemed like six months later they were gone. In many of those cases, they hadn't let God's Word put down roots in their hearts.

Most people don't like the root-building process. They want to experience the benefits that are visible in their lives, but they don't want to just spend time alone with God in His Word, letting it get rooted and established in them. That was a lesson I learned early on.

Sustaining Spiritual Growth

And he said, Whereunto shall we liken the kingdom of God? or with what comparison shall we compare it? It is like a grain of mustard seed, which, when it is sown in the earth, is less than all the seeds that be in the earth: but when it is sown, it groweth up, and becometh greater than all herbs, and shooteth out great branches; so that the fowls of the air may lodge under the shadow of it.

Mark 4:30–32

As I said earlier, while I was lying on my bunk in Vietnam, serving as bunker guard while everyone else was getting gassed, I used my time to get in the Word of God. I saw in this parable that the Lord was talking about growth, comparing it to a huge tree that spreads out until the birds of the air come and land in it. Jesus was saying that God sows a seed in your heart, and it grows. As it begins to produce, you begin ministering to other people and their lives are changed. As I was reading this and praying, I said, "God, this is what I want. I want you to touch my life and use me so I can touch people all over the world." I had no idea I'd be touching millions of people around the world through television and Charis Bible College, but I had the desire for it. So, I was just praying, "God, I want to be this huge tree that reaches out to touch and bless people."

And the Lord spoke to me and said, "If I were to answer your prayer today and give you this worldwide ministry that you desire, the first bird that landed on one of your branches would cause the whole thing to fall over, because your root is about an inch deep." The Lord went on to tell me to not worry about the growth above ground, but to put emphasis on getting rooted in the Word of God.

More than fifty years ago, God used this parable to teach me about the importance of the Word of God, and it gave me a track to run on. It gave me the direction to go.

I was in Vietnam for thirteen months, and for most of that time, I was by myself. I was a chaplain's assistant, and I only had a chaplain to serve for just a few months. The majority of the time, I was out on a fire support base away from the main bodies of the U.S. military, and there was really nothing to do.

On most days, I would study the Bible anywhere from ten to fifteen hours. In a practical sense, I actually stayed in a bunker for a while where I had to study the Word that long because it was wallpapered from ceiling to floor with pornographic pictures. I had to keep my Bible in front of my face the whole time just to make it!

Then, I'd pull bunker guard duty every single night just to have something to do, and I would sit and pray for four hours every night. Let me tell you, if you're not praying in tongues, you can pray for the whole world in thirty minutes! But I'd still just sit there and pray, meditating on God's Word.

So, that's at least ten hours in the Word and at least four hours praying every day for thirteen months. And it began to change my life.

Reaping a Harvest

Your heart is the ground. And when you got born again, God put in your heart everything that you will ever need.

For example, if you need finances, it's all in there. If you're born again, (Col. 2:10) you have the fullness of the Godhead in you bodily, and that includes finances. You just need to take the seed of God's Word and put it in your spiritual womb—your heart—and that seed will activate and conceive miracles.

You don't beg for miracles. You don't fast for miracles. You don't follow people around from conference to conference and let them lay on hands on you until you get your miracle. You conceive a miracle! It's as simple as conceiving a child.

Years ago, we were in a financial crisis. My wife, Jamie, and I had been tithing our entire lives, and we'd never had a dollar come our way that we didn't give from; so we understood some of the principles of prosperity. But our ministry was struggling. We couldn't pay our bills, got turned over to collection agencies all of the time, and it was bad. I would have to answer the phone because my staff just couldn't handle it. As a matter of fact, I had a board meeting where my board told me we were broke and that they were shutting down the ministry. So, we just decided to pray. And while we were praying, my mother called to tell me the ministry received a $60,000 gift in the mail that paid all of our debt and kept us going. But it was that way for many years. Our income just went up and down, and we struggled.

Yet, that whole time, the Lord was speaking to me that I was going to have a worldwide ministry. So, in 1996, I found about a hundred scriptures on prosperity, and I wrote them out longhand on a legal pad. I would just go through those scriptures, read them, pray over them, and meditate on them, using the same principles I'm teaching you in this booklet.

> You don't follow people around from conference to conference and let them lay on hands on you until you get your miracle. You conceive a miracle!

I did that for two years. And to most people there was no evidence of anything happening. But I was planting seed in my heart, meditating on it, and the earth—my heart—just brought forth fruit of herself

(Mark 4:28). All of a sudden, those seeds that I'd been sowing in my heart—they sprouted. Immediately, I got a revelation on finances!

Prior to that time, I'd been traveling and holding meetings, and the cost for each meeting was around $10,000. After we'd receive the offering, we would get something like $9,995 to $10,005. It seemed like we were within five or ten dollars of breaking even every time. Once I got that revelation though, the very next week I went to Arizona to hold a meeting. I didn't do anything different at that meeting, but when we received the offerings, about $24,000 came in—nearly two and a half times what we had been seeing before.

Since that time, the Lord has really blessed this ministry, but it's not because I've learned how to manipulate people or to do something. It's because I took the Word of God and meditated on it, and it has conceived prosperity.

Just a few years later, on July 26, 1999, the Lord woke me up early in the morning and said, "The time has come." I sat up and asked, "The time for what has come?" Then, the Lord revealed to me that the time to start my ministry had come.

Even though I had been in ministry nearly my entire adult life, the Lord was telling me it was time to *start* my ministry. And within a year, we were on television. Within ten years, we began moving forward on our Bible college campus in Woodland Park. We are touching millions, and potentially billions, of people around the world. Now, I'm not bragging on me, but I am bragging on what the Lord has done. It's all because I spent time sowing the seeds of God's Word in my heart, putting down roots that would support the vision God had for my life, and seeing it conceived and birthed into a worldwide ministry. Praise the Lord!

Conclusion

The Word of God is like a seed, and when you plant a seed, it's miraculous what happens. But if you just leave the seeds somewhere, they won't sprout until you plant them in the ground. Our heart is the ground. You may have heard me say this before, but I'm not the sharpest knife in the drawer. I had a guy introduce me once, and he said, "Andrew has never been accused of being the smartest person in the room."

I didn't take offense at that, but it's true! I'm just not the brightest, smartest, or most polished person. But the one thing I've done is to take God's Word and let it produce miraculous results for me and through me. My whole life and ministry are the product of meditating on God's Word. Any good thing in my life or ministry can be traced back to how God's Word has changed me. I believe it can be the same for you.

And as I've shared these truths in the Bible, I've seen hundreds of thousands of people's lives changed by the Word of God. I'm telling you, this is awesome!

Dirt is miraculous! And if you take the time to sow God's Word, you'll see the miraculous happen in your life too!

FURTHER STUDY

The truth will make you free (John 8:32), but it's only the truth you know that sets you free. What you don't know is hindering you. If you enjoyed this booklet and would like to learn more about some of the things I've shared, I suggest my other teachings:

- *Plain as Dirt*
- *Effortless Change*
- *A Sure Foundation*
- *The Power of Imagination*
- And my *Living Commentary* (online Bible software)

These teachings are available either free of charge at **awmi.net/video**, **awmi.net/audio**, or for purchase in book, study guide, CD, DVD, or USB formats at **awmi.net/store**.

Receive Jesus as Your Savior

Choosing to receive Jesus Christ as your Lord and Savior is the most important decision you'll ever make!

God's Word promises, *"That if thou shalt confess with thy mouth the Lord Jesus, and shalt believe in thine heart that God hath raised him from the dead, thou shalt be saved. For with the heart man believeth unto righteousness; and with the mouth confession is made unto salvation"* (Rom. 10:9–10). *"For whosoever shall call upon the name of the Lord shall be saved"* (Rom. 10:13). By His grace, God has already done everything to provide salvation. Your part is simply to believe and receive.

Pray out loud: "Jesus, I acknowledge that I've sinned and need to receive what you did for the forgiveness of my sins. I confess that You are my Lord and Savior. I believe in my heart that God raised You from the dead. By faith in Your Word, I receive salvation now. Thank You for saving me."

The very moment you commit your life to Jesus Christ, the truth of His Word instantly comes to pass in your spirit. Now that you're born again, there's a brand-new you!

Please contact us and let us know that you've prayed to receive Jesus as your Savior. We'd like to send you some free materials to help you on your new journey. Call our Helpline: **719-635-1111** (available 24 hours a day, seven days a week) to speak to a staff member who is here to help you understand and grow in your new relationship with the Lord.

Welcome to your new life!

Receive the Holy Spirit

As His child, your loving heavenly Father wants to give you the supernatural power you need to live a new life. *"For every one that asketh receiveth; and he that seeketh findeth; and to him that knocketh it shall be opened… how much more shall* your *heavenly Father give the Holy Spirit to them that ask him?"* (Luke 11:10–13).

All you have to do is ask, believe, and receive! Pray this: "Father, I recognize my need for Your power to live a new life. Please fill me with Your Holy Spirit. By faith, I receive it right now. Thank You for baptizing me. Holy Spirit, You are welcome in my life."

Some syllables from a language you don't recognize will rise up from your heart to your mouth (1 Cor. 14:14). As you speak them out loud by faith, you're releasing God's power from within and building yourself up in the spirit (1 Cor. 14:4). You can do this whenever and wherever you like.

It doesn't really matter whether you felt anything or not when you prayed to receive the Lord and His Spirit. If you believed in your heart that you received, then God's Word promises you did. *"Therefore I say unto you, What things soever ye desire, when ye pray, believe that ye receive them, and ye shall have them"* (Mark 11:24). God always honors His Word—believe it!

We would like to rejoice with you, pray with you, and answer any questions to help you understand more fully what has taken place in your life!

Please contact us to let us know that you've prayed to be filled with the Holy Spirit and to request the book *The New You & the Holy Spirit*. This book will explain in more detail about the benefits of being filled with the Holy Spirit and speaking in tongues. Call our Helpline: **719-635-1111** (available 24 hours a day, seven days a week).

Call for Prayer

If you need prayer for any reason, you can call our Helpline, 24 hours a day, seven days a week at **719-635-1111**. A trained prayer minister will answer your call and pray with you.

Every day, we receive testimonies of healings and other miracles from our Helpline, and we are ministering God's nearly-too-good-to-be-true message of the Gospel to more people than ever. So, I encourage you to call today!

About the Author

Andrew Wommack's life was forever changed the moment he encountered the supernatural love of God on March 23, 1968. As a renowned Bible teacher and author, Andrew has made it his mission to change the way the world sees God.

Andrew's vision is to go as far and deep with the Gospel as possible. His message goes far through the *Gospel Truth* television program, which is available to over half the world's population. The message goes deep through discipleship at Charis Bible College, headquartered in Woodland Park, Colorado. Founded in 1994, Charis has campuses across the United States and around the globe.

Andrew also has an extensive library of teaching materials in print, audio, and video. More than 200,000 hours of free teachings can be accessed at **awmi.net**.

Endnotes

1. David Barton, "Biblical Literacy," (presentation, Truth & Liberty Coalition Conference), September 9, 2022, accessed February 13, 2023, https://www.gospeltruth.tv/watch/?list=63175dbee9b2410001716d5c&id=631bc00dccd4240001f7e429.

2. "Pastors Face Communication Challenges in a Divided Culture," Barna Research Group, January 29, 2019, accessed February 21, 2023, https://www.barna.com/research/pastors-speaking-out/.

3. *Brown-Driver-Briggs Hebrew and English Lexicon*, s.v. "הָגָה" ("haga"), accessed February 13, 2023, https://www.blueletterbible.org/lexicon/h1897/kjv/wlc/0-1/.

4. *Thayer's Greek-English Lexicon of the New Testament*, s.v. "σπορά" ("spora"), accessed February 16, 2023, https://www.blueletterbible.org/lexicon/g4701/kjv/tr/0-1/.

5. *Thayer's Greek-English Lexicon of the New Testament*, s.v. "σπέρμα" ("sperma"), accessed February 16, 2023, https://www.blueletterbible.org/lexicon/g4690/kjv/tr/0-1/.

6. Laura Clark, "Tree Grown From 2,000-Year-Old Seed Has Reproduced," *Smithsonian Magazine*, March 26, 2015, accessed February 21, 2023, https://www.smithsonianmag.com/smart-news/tree-grown-2000-year-old-seed-has-reproduced-180954746/.

7. *Strong's Exhaustive Concordance*, s.v. "αὐτόματος" ("autómatos"), accessed March 27, 2023, https://www.blueletterbible.org/lexicon/g844/kjv/tr/0-1/.

Contact Information

Andrew Wommack Ministries, Inc.

PO Box 3333
Colorado Springs, CO 80934-3333
info@awmi.net
awmi.net

Helpline: 719-635-1111 (available 24/7)

Charis Bible College

info@charisbiblecollege.org
844-360-9577
CharisBibleCollege.org

For a complete list of all of our offices,
visit **awmi.net/contact-us**.

Connect with us on social media.